Thistle and Her First Day

Lady Thistle, the Horse

D.H. ANDERSON
Illustrations by STEVEN LESTER

Thistle and Her First Day

Paperback ISBN 978-1-960007-07-0
HardBack ISBN 978-1-960007-08-7
eBOOK ISBN 978-1-960007-09-4

Published by
Little Blessing Books
an imprint of
Orison Publishers, Inc.
PO Box 188, Grantham, PA 17027
www.OrisonPublishers.com

Acknowledgments

Contributing Artist: A. Newman
Contributing Veterinarian: Apryle Horbal, VMD

Waterdam Farm is a quiet and peaceful place where horses, cats, and a dog roam and play.

But tonight, on a cool, early spring evening, something is different; something very special has just happened.

Polly, a retired racehorse, has just given birth to a baby horse, a foal.

The tiny, long-legged, newborn baby horse is a filly, a little girl, and the Waterdam Farm family decides her name is Lady Thistle.

Things in the stable have changed; things at the farm will never be the same! But the other animal friends know this is a good change! A very special time!

The adventures of Lady Thistle begin!

What an exciting night in the barn at Waterdam Farm. Polly is a new MOM!

Her newborn baby, Lady Thistle, lies at her feet, still very wet from the birth. This small creature is quite different than the other horses.

Dr. Apryle and the family see that all seems to be good. Lady Thistle immediately tries to see what is going on around her.

Extra bedding of sawdust and straw has been added to the stall floor to make it nice and soft so Lady Thistle can rest and feel safe. The new foal's nose is very busy. She is getting her first smell of fresh cedar sawdust, sweet cut hay, and her mother's comforting scent.

Dr. Apryle, a veterinarian, tells the family that baby horses need to drink milk soon after being born, and the "first milk" from the mom is very important to keep baby horses from getting sick. Babies must drink it (nurse) in the first thirty minutes after they are born. Apryle immediately begins to figure out how to help Lady Thistle get up so she can stand to drink Polly's first milk.

But Lady Thistle is thinking only about what is going on around her. She hears the sounds of the other horses munching on their hay and dipping into their water buckets.

She begins to struggle, wanting to get up, wanting to see the other animals.

Every so often, the other horses stop munching and stretch their necks out over their stall guards to look toward Polly's stall, nickering and hoping to get a glimpse of the new foal. They are very excited, very curious, and are eager to welcome her to their cozy living space.

Baby Thistle is tired and again lying still beside her mom, but she continues to hear the sounds of the other horses and wants to see what is going on. Polly is up and prepared for Thistle to nurse.

Dr. Apryle knows that Thistle's quiet time must be interrupted.

She wants this baby horse to drink right away. First, the wet filly must get up–she must try to stand on her long, wobbly legs. Baby Thistle is having a hard time figuring out how to stand. Maybe she needs some help.

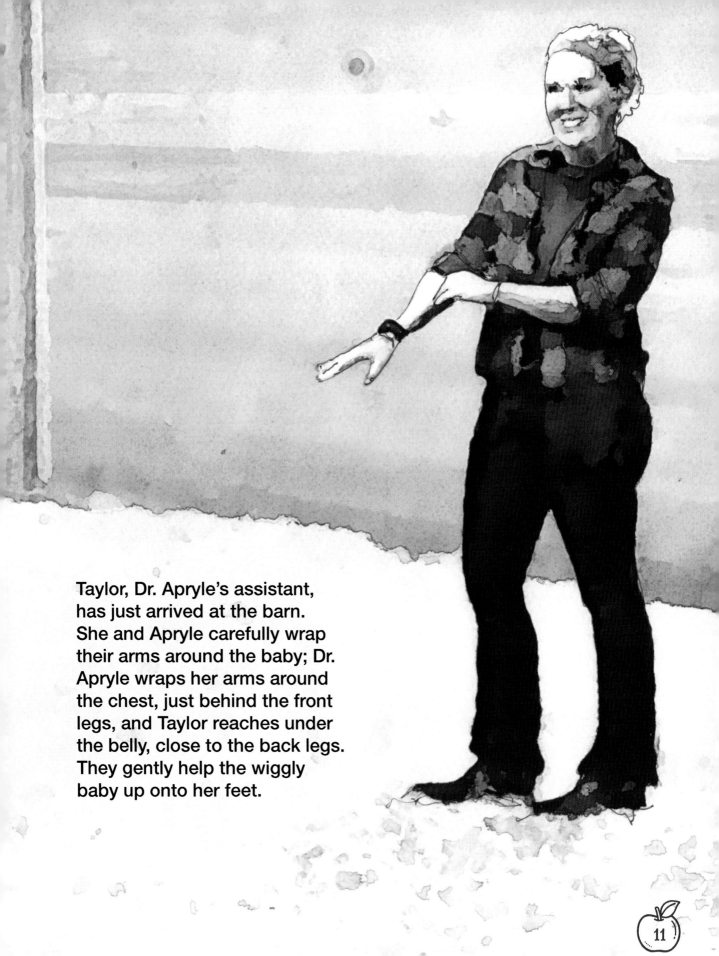

Taylor, Dr. Apryle's assistant, has just arrived at the barn. She and Apryle carefully wrap their arms around the baby; Dr. Apryle wraps her arms around the chest, just behind the front legs, and Taylor reaches under the belly, close to the back legs. They gently help the wiggly baby up onto her feet.

At first, tiny Thistle loses her balance. Her legs are too long, and they are not sturdy. Dr. Apryle and Taylor hang on tight! Then, after a few minutes, Thistle finds her balance and can stand!

Taylor then gently guides Thistle's nose toward Polly's udder. But Thistle is still not interested in eating. She wants to look all around, not to put her nose under Polly's belly. There is just so much to see!

She again hears the other horses and wobbles toward the open stall door.

Dr. Apryle and Taylor quickly move to keep her in. They are worried that little Thistle will escape!

Thistle needs to nurse, but she just wants to explore!

So, what can they do?

The curious cats and Yanik, the farm dog, hear exciting sounds coming from the horse barn and arrive to meet Thistle. Thistle sticks her nose out into the aisle of the barn to meet her new friends. The cats scatter when they first see her. But slowly, they come back. Yanik decides his place is to guard the door of the barn.

14

All this activity does not help Thistle think about her mother's milk. Dr. Apryle is worried. Sometimes a mother horse does not care about having her baby nurse. Sometimes a baby horse is born too soon and is just not ready for nursing.

But Thistle just needs to pay attention.

Polly knows that Thistle MUST DRINK! She nickers for Thistle to come close, but Thistle has other things she wants to see.

Thistle must not wait any longer. Aunt Daphne decides it is time
to help. She stretches her head out of the stall, looks across the
aisle to Thistle, and nickers firmly, telling Thistle to listen to her
mom and drink her milk–NOW!

This time when Dr. Apryle and Taylor guide the baby's nose toward Polly, the newborn latches on and begins to drink her mother's special milk eagerly.

She is very HUNGRY! She has used so much of her energy being born!

18

Polly gently nuzzles her new little girl as she nurses. Polly is a great mom, and she stands patiently while Thistle figures out how to drink from the udder. Sometimes Thistle nibbles a bit too hard on Polly, but with a firm reminder, Polly lets her know how to drink gently. There are two udder openings, and Thistle learns to use both. Luckily, Thistle has no teeth yet!

MMMMMM!

21

This milk from the mother is the only food a newborn horse needs. It contains vitamins and protein. Most importantly, it has colostrum to protect the baby from getting sick while she is very young.

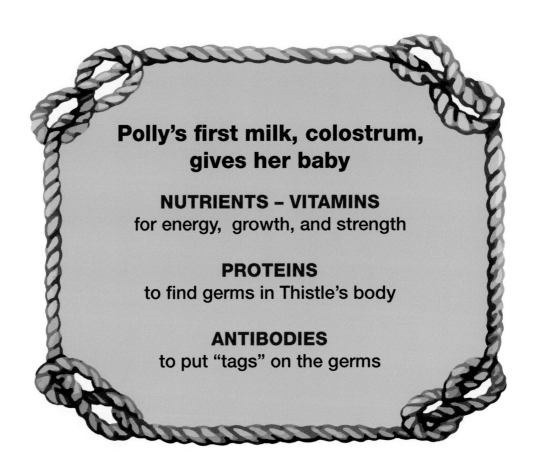

Polly's first milk, colostrum, gives her baby

NUTRIENTS – VITAMINS
for energy, growth, and strength

PROTEINS
to find germs in Thistle's body

ANTIBODIES
to put "tags" on the germs

This helps Thistle get rid of the tagged germs quickly until she has her own **IMMUNE SYSTEM**.

Baby Thistle gets

no fragrant hay,

no tasty grain,

no sweet green grass…

YET.

Polly's instincts tell her what a new baby horse needs. Now that Thistle has had her milk, the new mom gently licks her little baby all over until she is clean and dry.

Both Mom and baby are now very tired, and they lie down to rest. They have worked very hard tonight. Polly cannot stop nuzzling her new little Thistle. And Thistle feels warm and safe lying next to her mom.

The family, Dr. Apryle, and Taylor leave the barn knowing that nature will take over!

All is quiet, except for the soothing, continuous munching of hay…

Did You Know...?

The immune system is what fights off disease in horses, people, and all other animals. As the baby horse grows, its immune system learns how to fight against diseases.

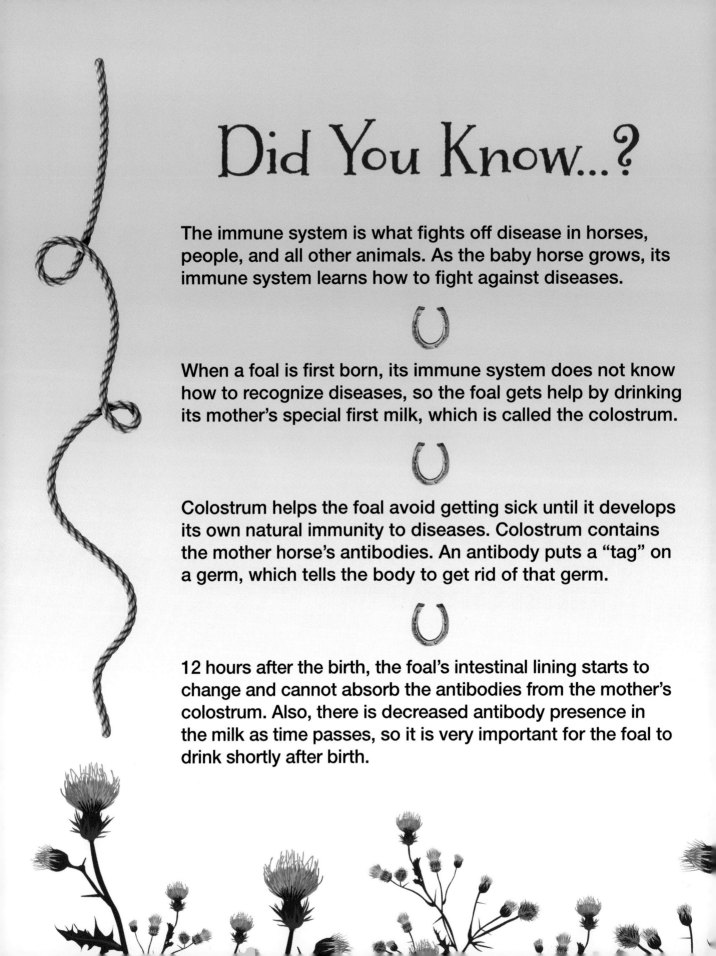

When a foal is first born, its immune system does not know how to recognize diseases, so the foal gets help by drinking its mother's special first milk, which is called the colostrum.

Colostrum helps the foal avoid getting sick until it develops its own natural immunity to diseases. Colostrum contains the mother horse's antibodies. An antibody puts a "tag" on a germ, which tells the body to get rid of that germ.

12 hours after the birth, the foal's intestinal lining starts to change and cannot absorb the antibodies from the mother's colostrum. Also, there is decreased antibody presence in the milk as time passes, so it is very important for the foal to drink shortly after birth.

These are some big words for some very small but important parts of the mother's milk. One little germ can make a baby horse very sick, but one little antibody can fight it off!

The foal should stand up within about thirty minutes after being born and can walk steadily in a few hours. This allows the foal to stand and drink the mother's milk.

If a foal is too weak and does not nurse, it may be necessary to milk the mom (like a cow is milked) and give the colostrum to the foal. If the mom does not have enough milk, a backup supply can be found.

The foal should have a special blood test done when it is about one day old to make sure the antibodies are in its blood and able to do their job. If not, a veterinarian can help by giving the foal some extra blood containing super-charged antibodies.

It is important when caring for a new foal that you be calm, prepared, and learn how to help the mother and baby get off to a good start. It's important to work with a vet and have a plan to assist the foal if it has any trouble.

Coming Soon!

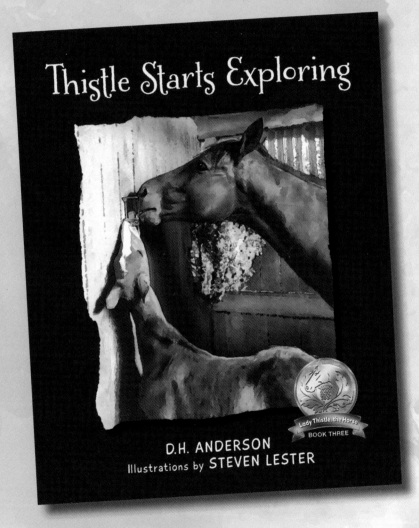

Thistle Starts Exploring

D.H. ANDERSON
Illustrations by STEVEN LESTER

Lady Thistle, the Horse
BOOK THREE

Watch

for the

Next Book

in the

Series

SCAN ME

Read more stories as young Thistle grows.